LITTLE BLUE
READERS

Making
a Car

Focus: Systems

PETER SLOAN &
SHERYL SLOAN

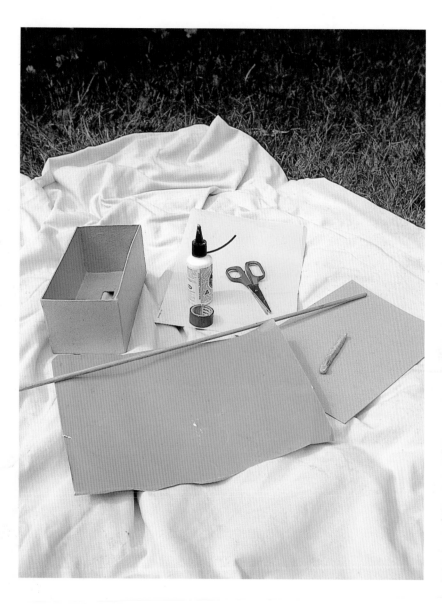

A car is made of
many parts.

Make a body for people to ride in.

Add some wheels
to move it on
the road.

Add a steering
wheel to steer
the car.

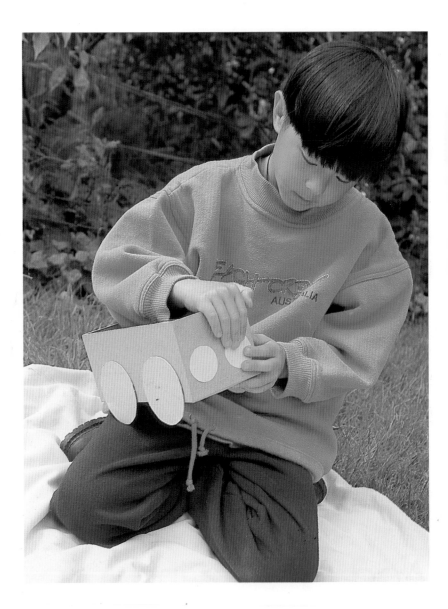

Add some lights
to see at night.

Put a driver in
the car.

The driver is ready
to drive away.